Blue Rooms

I0152723

Blue Rooms

Morri Creech

WAYWISER

First published in 2018 by

THE WAYWISER PRESS

Christmas Cottage, Church Enstone, Chipping Norton, Oxfordshire, OX7 4NN, UK
P.O. Box 6205, Baltimore, MD 21206, USA
https://waywiser-press.com

Editor-in-Chief
Philip Hoy

Senior American Editor
Joseph Harrison

Associate Editors
Eric McHenry | Dora Malech | V. Penelope Pelizzon | Clive Watkins
Greg Williamson | Matthew Yorke

A CIP catalogue record for this book is available from the British Library

Paperback ISBN: 978-1-904130-92-5
Hardback ISBN: 978-1-904130-93-2

Printed and bound by
Ingram / Lightning Source

for Miriam

Acknowledgements

Hopkins Review: "History: a Tour of the Grounds"
Missouri Review: sections 1, 2, 6, 9, 10, 12, and 13 of "Still Life"
The New Criterion: "Magpies at the Sea," "At Buck Hall"
Oxford American: "The Confession"
Prairie Schooner: "Self-Portrait as Magritte," "Self-Portrait after Goya"
Smartish Pace: "The Bronze Stairwell," sections 3, 4, 5, 8, and 11 of "Still Life"
Southwest Review: "The Language of Pastoral," "Tōhaku's Folding Screen"
Yale Review: "Cézanne"

"Some Notes on Grace and Gravity" originally appeared in *Field Knowledge* (Waywiser Press, 2006).

Thanks to Queens University of Charlotte for its support during the writing of this book; and special thanks to Sarah Creech, Joseph Harrison, and Michael Shewmaker for their suggestions and advice in shaping it.

The following poems are dedicated to the following individuals: "Self-Portrait as Magritte" to Joshua Mehigan; "The Language of Pastoral" to Susan Ludvigson; "Magpies at the Sea" to Sarah Creech; "The Bronze Stairwell" to Michael Kobre; and "At Buck Hall" to the memory of Scott Ely.

Table of Contents

"Everything we see hides another thing, we always want to see what is hidden by what we see."

— René Magritte

Self-Portrait as Magritte

1.

I am the son of man, Magritte,
The one in bowler hat and coat
Who walks behind you on the street,
A tie fixed firmly at his throat.

I am the footsteps following you,
The no one that is always there,
The stranger on the avenue
Advancing toward the silent square.

I am the absence in the curtain
Through which you see the sea and sky,
The doubt you feel when things look certain,
The truth behind your alibi.

2.

Beneath a triple moon, three men
Stand in the wasteland outside town.
It's nearly dark at half past ten.
Two look away. One wears a frown.

The world beyond is cold and bare
But set against a distant light.
There are no shadows anywhere.
The houses vanish out of sight.

These three men share my look and dress.
I cannot say which one is me.
Three ways I face the emptiness,
The central man, the mystery.

3.

My mother drowned when I was young.
In dreams sometimes I see her face.
I wring my hands but hold my tongue
And stare off into empty space.

There are some things you can't erase.
The dress pulled just above her head
Reveals a hem of Belgian lace.
I've never seen a thing so dead.

I wake. The world is not the same.
Why should I paint what's merely true?
And what is art? A serious game
I play alone. And just for you.

4.

No one actually believes
The red sun fixed on a dark tree,
The men who fall like autumn leaves,
The face that, turned, still looks at me;

No one believes the clouds at noon
Scudding through a cut-out bird,
The candle cup that holds a moon,
The pipe whose caption word for word

Gives the lie to what it seems.
But isn't illusion half the truth—
That silhouette I see in dreams
And worry like a missing tooth?

5.

One day the dead will disappear.
We will not see them anymore.
One day all the clouds will clear
And waves break on an empty shore.

I limn a strange identity.
The face I wear on every street
Looks just like the one you see
Hanging on the real Magritte.

I paint it just to please my whim.
It's best to laugh and not to weep.
At night I see my mother's hem
And the river lays me down to sleep.

6.

The kissing lovers' shrouded heads
Lean together in ignorance:
So all are strangers in their beds
According to the evidence.

The vision rarely comes out right.
A quirk lurks in the commonplace.
The day peeks through the scrim of night
And a white bird obscures my face.

Where have all the shadows gone?
They crowd around the mirror frame.
I stare up at the fruit of dawn.
You look at me. We are the same.

7.

This, then, is my final word,
Last testament of René Magritte
Who paints the rare and the absurd.
I walk along the cobbled street

And say the man that turns from you
Is different than you may suppose.
He stares off at the distant blue,
The gentleman nobody knows.

Picasso had his blue guitar,
Dalí his clocks. I tell no lies.
I paint the strangers that we are.
The self is still our best disguise.

The Language of Pastoral

1.

I am halfway between the canebrake and the pines.
The horizon stretches like a bow-string, sun
Deep citron over the pasture. Language whines
And lisps toward meaning, trying to get one
Blessèd thing right—O wonders turned to signs:
Trees shine with mold out where the creekbeds run,
Wet fields brim with midges, and white curds
Of foam wash up at the pond's edge in these words.

2.

Like spells to conjure with, this verb, this noun—
Three red-winged blackbirds at the pasture's edge
Gleaning the grass seed have already flown
And disappeared somewhere beyond the hedge,
Only to be recalled in this phrase, set down
As a part of speech. So language keeps its pledge.
I find the loss in what these words redeem,
Like the sleeper who awakes to another dream.

3.

I have come back in the middle of a sentence
In middle life: here my grandfather tended
Corn and plowed the back fields, stripped the dense
Kudzu before it choked the soybeans. Winded,
He'd walk along the full length of the fence
To drink cold water where the creekbed ended.
I imagine seeing him climb the distant hill.
Language sings its one song, *hold still, hold still.*

4.

What I have to say turns the pasture to fiction.
Parsing the back fields, grammar and syntax fail.
Even the blackbirds are reduced to diction,
Sculling through air as they do above the swale.
A world combusts to nothing in the friction
Between a phrase and its referent: or the tale
Persists as cadence, though the names of things
Are frail as spent breath or the midges' wings.

5.

Whom or what are these words for? Not the dead
Who cannot hear them anyway. Not the wet
Soybean fields or canebrake or the red-
Winged blackbirds slurring the air. What slips the net
Of language has no use for what is said
About it. Even I will soon forget.
Each word quarrels with silence at the close:
Where speech comes from, and where everything goes.

6.

It is dark as I write this. The fields are far away.
Maybe the pasture hums with midges, reeds
Teem at my grandfather's fenceline, and a stray
Blackbird lifts toward the hill, beak full of seeds.
Maybe, for all the words I have had to say,
Someone sits alone in a room and reads
In silence a poem beginning with these lines:
I am halfway between the canebrake and the pines …

Magpies at the Sea

I remember three magpies on the beach
Chasing the foam. The day was blue.

They pecked at something out of reach
Beyond the tide pool's edge and flew.

I can't be sure how much is true.
Sun glinting from a sea grape leaf,

A palm's green shadow on the strand
Are now a matter of belief.

I say those scholars of the sand
Circled above the distant reef

Much as a thought circles the mind,
Circles and will not relent.

Whatever it was they hoped to find,
Those strangers to that element,

They disappeared beyond the sea
(Then several times in memory)

Like a cloud on the horizon does,
Or thread unravels from its clew;

The way that *is* slips into *was*;
The way that *know* turns into *knew*.

Cézanne

1.

The man with brush and palette knife
Watches the gleaming light of Aix.
A scrim of cloud goes skimming by.
If it is a solitary life
To paint with brush and palette knife
The spheres, the cones, and cylinders
Of nature in a layered light,
Then this is the man and these the right
Structures and geometric shapes
To see things by. The colors shift
Beneath the essences distilled
Of mountain, orange, pine, or peach.
The world and his perception rhyme
On a canvas of arrested time.

2.

An ancient sun has shed its blue.
Here the wind goes slow, then still,
Beneath a smear of deeper brown
On rooftops at the edge of town.
A balding man stands on the hill.
He sees the sea, shades it the hue
Of consciousness, with strokes of white,
One island like a far meringue.
To set things down the way they seem
And get the sullen colors right,
Shape of a woman's folded hands
Or oranges wrapped in swaddling bands,
Those stray folds where the shadows start,
Are all his labor and his art.

3.

Paint the colors, paint them on
The quiet hills at dusk or dawn.
Paint Harlequin and Pierrot.
Whatever else the angels do,
None whispers in a bishop's ear
Or crowds by an important chair.
None wears a father's leather shoe.
They do not natter in the blue
Of ordinary fields. The mind
Grows anxious in its search to find
Some meaning in the daub of day.
When the paint of thought is scraped away
It reveals not the world we know
But another, deeper, just below.

4.

Celestial things have no place here.
The commonest will do: a pear,
A bottle, two eggs, a loaf of bread,
A man whose beard and sober head
Display the changes of the year.
He shifts a bit to adjust his view,
The man with brush and palette knife,
In a world of shifting constancies.
Though in the teeth of time and change
He has managed to arrange
Permanent shapes that will outlast
The subjects that decay so fast,
His apples rot as the paint dries.
He hears the buzzing of the flies.

5.

The real is what we think it is:
Melting snow at Fontainebleau,
Lavender touched by morning dew.
It is a man in a white-stained cap
Who holds his brushes in his lap
And works to make his vision true.
But atoms in the clearest air
Compose the easel and the chair
Where he paints, that man from Aix.
Each brushstroke makes it seem as though
Aqueduct, garden, and chateau
Are motions in a stillness, bare
And rinsed, a smutch of white and green,
Until one sorts what one has seen.

6.

Sensation is the aim of thought.
It is a matter for the eye
That one's perspective alters sky
From gray to cobalt by device,
That one can see the same thing twice,
Three, no, a hundred times, and note
A difference in the dusky hues
Each time the pupil takes it in.
Let's paint the familiar thing again.
Let's watch the steel blue at L'Estaque
Become, on second glance, the black
Of heavy clouds, late winter, when
Perception sees the shapes unwind
Before they reach the shaping mind.

7.

An atmosphere of autumn light
Against a backdrop of green pines,
Old woman with a rosary,
A bather slumped against a tree,
The chateau on the hill at night
Are all a part of his designs,
The man from Aix. He shuts his eyes.
And what he sees is past surmise.
Behind the eyelids' crucial dark,
The imagined and the real
Blend to what we think and feel.
He blinks and makes a final mark.
Shapes appear as they appear.
The shadows, lengthening, grow near.

The Bronze Stairwell

There is a bronze stairwell that curves beyond
The rooms of thought and feeling, toward the thing
Itself, toward that veranda where the actual
Persimmons ripen next to the effusions
Of sunlight at the railing. This stairwell leads
Downward into the basement of abstraction
As leptons, quarks, and bosons speed and whirl
To science's dazzlement and profound confusion,
As matter plays a host to emptiness
And emptiness takes matter in its arms
Like a lover stepping from her satin dress.
The bronze stairwell leads everywhere and nowhere.
It rises to the locked room down the hallway,
The room we know exists though we can't see,
Whose very furniture gives matter shape
(Like the chaise that curves the body as it curves)
And on whose wall the clock keeps telling time.
The stairwell turns beyond the rooms of thought
And yet it takes the mind, as Berkeley knew,
To conjure matter purely through perception—
Matter thinking itself and understanding
As much as a thing can understand itself
And thinking, too, of what cannot be thought,
Thinking the steep floors that it can't ascend,
That spiral up beyond the spinning planets
And down into the detonating atom,
Matter thinking and hearing itself think
And hearing, or thinking it hears, from time to time,
The sound of someone's footsteps on the stairs.

Some Notes on Grace and Gravity

1. Giotto

The postured myths of Byzantines? Ho-hum.
Leave Cimabue the manner and the gaze
Of saints whose sandals never bore their weight,
Their very gowns stunned to beatitude—
But if two men kiss at Gethsemane
There should be torchlight and the crush of mobs,
A keen blade raised to glance the soldier's ear.
Let there be lutes and fiddles to attend
The virgin's marriage; or, say, at the gate
Where Anna and Joachim may sometime meet,
The common stir and gossiping of girls.
Saints in their figured scenes will stand before
The fur of shepherds' boots, the dogs and sheep,
And there will be much fidgeting of gowns
Amid the old hosannas, the solid heft
And weight of angels' wings to brush the ground.

2. Leonardo

Christ at the table, Mary among the rocks.
A grace, he knew, lay hidden in their limbs
That lay, too, in the limbs of criminals,
The twist and torque of carpenters' bare shoulders,
Even the faces of his ugly children—
When asked why his own offspring looked so poor
Compared to the rich productions of his brush,
He'd once replied, "I make paintings by day,
Children at night." And it had been at night
In a church basement, one old story goes,
That the artist set aside his brush and palette,
Lifted a surgeon's knife above the table,
And found the grace that hangmen share with saints
Lay not in the spirit's quickenings and motion
But stretched out in the sinews' long striations,
In webbed integument and the curve of bone.

3. Newton

A minor disappointment not to find
Angels pushing the planets around their courses
As Leibniz believed. A shame, but not a great one,
That the universe seemed less and less to hang
Glimmering from God's chain like a golden fob,
Although a pendent weight shaped Newton's thought.

Sitting alone there in that storied orchard,
He'd seen the apples drooping on their boughs;
Until one formed, unplucked, a grand conclusion.
The apple fell because it had to fall,
As objects move toward objects, in accord.
It struck a dizzying tune into his head.

The clockwork of the heavens may make music,
But it was a grave music that he heard,
The whirl of mass, the hum of centrifuge,
And calculations on the page would prove
Such motion both a falling and a flight.
Thus bodies spin each other round in space.

And gravity, too, becomes a kind of grace.

At Buck Hall

1.

Like dipping oars the egret strikes its wings
On the estuary out near Pimlico,
Scanning for those widening, dimpled rings
Where fish break water, talons skimming low
Over the shoals. An itch for landscape brings
Me back here to these wetlands in the slow
Half light of afternoon. Loose threads of day
Spin themselves out in what I have to say.

2.

To shape coherence from that far company—
Harrier hawk circling above the swales,
White tail scrambling across the thorns and scree
Of the slick limestone berm. My eyesight fails
To knit it whole. Unlike the owl in its tree
That sees the least twitch in the swaying cattails,
I patch together buck, scree, briar, and bird
As best I can in the clear light, word by word.

3.

Such distance between what the eye takes in
And what the tongue gives back in its puzzle and sift,
Sorting the mayflies from the dazzled spin
Of oak leaves flashing silver. In the rift
Between idea and flesh a brown marsh wren
Flittering from a paper birch, too swift
For vision to hone in, grows still, having lit
Here in the space this phrase has made for it.

4.

Suppose the sayer changes what he sees,
Or makes a marsh wren up for story's sake
When a tanager, in fact, wings through the breeze
To cross the sawgrass shallows by the lake,
Having flown from a stand of fictive trees.
What if this word-stitched landscape is a fake?
For all my honest effort, lies are hidden
In the pretense of each sentence I have written.

5.

Think how the visible becomes a dream
When, by some quirk of thought, a beech leaf stirs
And turns into a fawn's ear, or a stream
Glints like a fish's scales. The mind conjures
The world to artifice, skews *be* to *seem*
In wild pursuit of meaning. What endures
—A paradigm in which the marsh wren flies—
Is truer still for being a disguise.

6.

The shank end of late afternoon goes on
About its business heedless of the sounds
Language has made of it. In a pond frogspawn
Festers and reeks. A hare near the levee bounds
Deep in the blackberry vines. When I am gone
Egret and hawk will carry on their rounds.
And so will I, at my desk, when the day has passed,
Setting it down in these words to make it last.

Near Wrightsville Beach

The gulls are circling the blue rooms of afternoon.
You can hear the waves scrawling on the shore
The ambiguous scripts of summer, indecipherable,
As jade spray leaps the boards to wet the deck.
It is the beginning and the end of structure,
The linking and the lack, the shape and breakage,
Like meaning woven out of its unweaving
Or the sky reflected and rucked in azure water.
In a green distance the sea composes itself
From all the discords thundering under the keel,
From a thousand fragments of its glittering
Piecemeal beneath the iris of the sun,
The way a conch shapes sound from the raw air
Or several notions knit a single knowledge
That is itself the jade spray and the shore,
The slick deck underfoot, the wind and water,
Sky and the marble majesty of clouds,
Until you stand above the rocking swells
And conceive a thought that reaches to the sun
Slowly evolving an image of its kind:
The gulls are circling the blue rooms of the mind.

Still Life

1.

The tragic undertones that mar our best achievements,
The sense, beneath the languor of afternoon, that things
Come to an end, that one moment falls into the next
And the footsteps of the past fade down the long hallway,
Have nothing to do with the pears at rest in their dish.
How still they are by the sugar bowl and tablecloth,
How poised for a conclusion that never comes, canted
Toward the foreground as if they could spill to the floor,
Though they never do. They are a trick of perception,
Of course, all curve and color, not the solid objects
That we take them to be. Time, in passing, has given
Them a sense of timelessness. They are lit from within.
They appear as pears, these shapes, pears of pure idea.

2.

When you think of the past, what comes to mind is the dead
Peacock you once saw hanging from the wall in winter,
The blood and claws and stiff wings and the dazzling plumage,
And later on how your father plucked and gutted it,
Rinsed the tender meat, then quartered it in the kitchen.
You were the girl in the light of the window who stared
And thought to herself: nothing has ever looked so still.
You were maybe nine or ten. But what you think of now,
More than the smells of the kitchen or the blood drying
On the stones, more than the way your father held the knife
Above the cutting board, whistling while the tendons snapped,
Is how you knew then that you would keep this memory
As you glimpsed yourself in the gleam of the peacock's eye.

3.

There are rooms you visit in the height of sleep that seem
Like museums of the mind, where you lean in to look.
Tonight you can see, arranged on a table whose thick
Tablecloth seduces the shadows, the coffee cup
Your grandmother drank from when she mused at the window
In winter, the conch you found on the beach as a child,
And the clock, hands missing, that sat on the mantelpiece
In the den, keeping its counsel those anxious minutes
You were made to wait though eager to be off and play.
Once, steam rose from the cup beside the kitchen sink, once
The conch shone in the shallows, but only the objects
Remain now, bereft of context, odd etceteras
That the mind preserves, timeless as a clock without hands.

4.

The good life may be merely this basket of apples
And oranges spilling out on the sensuous folds
Of a tablecloth, in summertime, the rich shadows
More like a revelation of light than a darkness
To be reckoned with, everything ripening toward
The consummation of color and shape and design,
Displayed for the delicate seduction of the eye,
Of the hand that longs for the curve and dimple of flesh
And the mind that savors simply by contemplating
The zest on the tongue, the texture of pulp at the pith,
The heaviness of fruit as it tumbles on the cloth
And satisfies in the very temptation, the thought
Of what lies just beyond our reach, of endless delight.

5.

How to put down in words the exact brilliance one finds
Around the gilt mirror and the majolica bowl
Next to which bristles this rich arrangement of flowers
In a blue vase? There is no language for light, which is
To painting as ideas are to literature,
And these objects are positioned merely to define
And heighten what cannot be seen except in contrast,
As the Cloud of Unknowing was once drawn between man
And God, the better to see Him by. Thus the shadows
Crowding the petals and the folds of the tablecloth,
Thus the slick polish in the luster of the mirror,
As though you could see yourself reflected in a light
Three centuries old, and beyond the reach of language.

6.

It has been observed before, of course, how oppressive
Is the stillness of painted plums and jugs and silver
Tureens to those who are caught in the flux of motion,
The failing of flesh into time. About the stasis
And Keatsian calm one finds in art—the idleness
Of the cat crouched next to the pheasant it cannot reach,
The noon sunlight flooding the kitchen window without
Diminishment—about that semblance of forever
I have nothing to add, standing behind the plush ropes
That keep me on this side of timelessness, the minutes
Bearing me slowly into a future where jugs break
And silver tarnishes, where plums molder in their dish,
Where the cat, pheasant caught in its mouth, leaps and is gone.

7.

Though fresh pears ripen on the table by the window,
Though it is August and the bowl is full, memory
Sets aside the present to recall the chill that held
A distant prospect of bloom and fruit. The past is still
A place where frost thickens on the pear trees and summer
Is a rumor. Now, amid sunlight and the longed-for
Warmth that had seemed so remote in the fruitless days when
Snow lay clean and even on the ground, the idea
Of winter conjures up the frozen hills and brittle
Ice-locked branches, January resurrects its old
Conspiracy of cold in the space behind the eyes,
And the season sounding out its windswept cadences
In the orchard of thought ripens with the dusky pears.

8.

In the past, sun shone on the lawn where your grandfather
Turned the torque wrench, loosening the bolts from the camshaft,
And set the parts down in the grass like a work of art.
It was a September morning and you were the boy
Standing underneath the dogwood, pronouncing the names,
Gasket, compressor, piston, crankcase, carburetor,
As oil spread its rainbow and leaves trembled in a wind
That carried this moment slowly toward the present
Where the man that you are now tries to set down in words
The engine parts splayed in the grass, the color of oil
And the look of the greased bolts held in the metal pan,
All caught in the cogs of time, in the teeth of the gears
That keep lurching forward, grinding the moments to dust.

9.

How instructive, the skull placed among the bric-a-brac,
Among all these objects arranged like a jumble sale:
The necklace tossed as an afterthought on the table
Where the book lies open to a page we cannot see
And the fluted glass, the loose change, and the pocket watch
Gleam in what spare light the painter has afforded us,
Saying, how fleeting is time, how futile is desire.
Here are plums and quinces, an apple halved on a plate,
Caught in their sumptuous tumble to oblivion,
And the violin waiting there, lovely but untouched,
Since no one comes to this seventeenth century room
Rendered in paint except to examine the riches,
While the skull looks back with its air of cool appraisal.

10.

Or take, for instance, this still life from a Pompeii wall
Of fruits and vases, grapes and cherries and apples heaped
High in a bowl so clear we can see to the bottom—
What astonishes me is not how well the painting
Handles its subject, how the ancient light suffuses
The trompe l'oeil shelves and the vase tipped slightly off kilter,
But how the ash of history sweeps its pluming cloud
Into the hush and calm of the domestic, how it
Sinters down in heavy drifts that cover everything,
Starting with a flake, small, merely a smutch on the palm,
Then the slow accumulation on streets and houses,
Sure as the gray in my hair or rising summer heat,
Burying art, too, darling of time, in its warm snows.

11.

Here, then, is my *vanitas*: farewell to the peaches
Left in the studio, rotten and crawling with flies.
Farewell to what does not endure, the flesh that loosens,
Bubbling and oozing on the table, in the basket,
As the colors dry on the canvas—Cézanne painted
So slowly that his flowers mottled and shriveled up
Before he could set them down. Farewell to the brushes
And palette, to the odds and ends in the studio,
And the painter himself with his beard and overalls.
Farewell to the nineteenth century, the twentieth
With its aggrieved, fractured art and its terrible wars,
Farewell to all who turn to art for its permanence,
And to the art itself, which lasts for a time, farewell.

12.

For weeks now I have been meditating on still lifes,
The tumble of plums and pears, the overturned goblets
And the sundry bouquets of flowers, the skulls and flutes.
I have grown bored with their quaintness and simplicity
And, well, their *stillness*, which lacks the narrative power
Of Christ's agony in the garden or the sublime
Force of Turner's slave ship, an alp or a starry night.
I tire of the repetitions of subject matter,
The endless spill of quinces, grapes, and pomegranates—
Though, child of time that I am, caught up in the thunder
And motion of history, I sometimes find comfort
In the calm seductions of pitcher and vase, shadow
And light, the modest raptures of the ordinary.

13.

The apples in the basket, the apples of the mind,
The apple grown so enormous that it fills a room,
Heaps of them set out on the great table by the sea,
Are not so much the fruit plucked in the fabled garden
Or held in the palm of Paris, gift to a goddess,
As they are a mode of thought, serene in their rondure
And repose, their being merely what they are, beyond
The evasion of metaphor, and beyond the fact
Of their actual ripeness, heaviness, and luster,
Not the bare thing with all of its flaws but the notion
Of the thing, shaken loose from the tree of idea
And placed in a room, piled high on a dish or table,
Like a dream of perfect form, arranged for you to see.

Tōhaku's Folding Screen

Consider this screen
Whose ghostly strew of pine trees,
   All shade and flourish

And slender line, fades
In a mist or fog implied
   By the feathered strokes

Of the artist's brush.
History is quiet here.
   One can hardly think

Of villages razed
To splinters and seething ash,
   Or crops set afire.

Elsewhere, of course, men
Slay each other for honor.
   Elsewhere the jinkai

Blow on fields covered
With corpses. But here the pines
   Leaning from the mist

Conjure a stillness
So delicate, when you fold
   The screen it is gone.

History: A Tour of the Grounds

1.

Clattering sounds of the carriage wheels repeat.
Cement-braced oak trees bristle in strict rows,
Their parallels narrowing in retreat
The way the years come slowly to a close
Or Something and Nothing gradually meet
(What happens after that nobody knows
Though it is said one only has to wait).
The dirt road leads to the preserved estate.

2.

This is the table where the peace was signed.
Here is the room where whispers led to blood.
Shelves of the great man's library are lined
With manuscripts that date before the flood
And drafts of the symphony he finished blind.
The wall was built with oyster shells and mud.
Each year a small piece of the story goes,
Claimed by the ivy and the climbing rose.

3.

Plinths. Doric columns. Quoins and architraves.
Behind plush ropes the gilded, too-short bed
And the chair that held an Earl upright. Sun laves
The mullioned panes to polychrome. The dead
Are posed in portrait frames, far from the graves,
Kept from the lesser things they did and said.
Muse of meaning, color with fresh tints
The lives that survive their first significance.

4.

There are vast mansions in our fathers' house.
Not everyone stays at the storied end
To duel beneath the chandelier, carouse
Among the hedgerows dandled by the wind,
And die at hearthside next to dog or spouse
(A shaky fact the scholars may amend).
Still, most of us would visit here again.
The tour guide smiles and gladly waves us in.

The Confession

I could draw you a picture if I had a mind to.
Out past the last road there were woods and a still.

There were cars in front of a ramshackle barn,
The moon in a cloud and a tree on the hill.

I remember the raw December weather,
Boys shouting curses and most of them drunk.

I remember the wind in the barley stubble.
I remember the man they dragged from the trunk.

The moon appeared and disappeared.
Headlights and whiskey. A tree on the hill.

We tied the knot and we threw it over.
It took half an hour for his legs to go still.

Just boys, for all that, in December weather,
Settling a grievance, correcting a wrong.

I remember one shoe kicked off in the heather.
I remember my feet hurt from standing so long.

The place may be there. I could draw you a picture.
The moon in a cloud and a tree on the hill.

Damned if I know how I see it so clearly.
Don't ask me to speak of it. Damned if I will.

Self-Portrait after Goya

When Goya lifts his brush to paint my nightmare
He steadies his right hand and doesn't speak.
I cannot move, strapped to my fever chair.
He makes a mark. And then I know the meek
Will not inherit the kingdom or the kind
Be blessed as in some Sunday homily . . .
When Goya paints my dream, I see God grind
Children to bits in his maw, I see the tree
On which a corpse is skewered through the ass
And hangs dismembered, dead fish in a heap,
And witches stripped to celebrate black mass
Until you wake me up, I start from sleep
Thrashing as though I were about to drown,
And Goya, finished, puts his paint brush down.

2.

Sometimes at night I dream that I am Goya
Painting the Spanish king in hunting clothes,
Condesa de Chinchón in her gold chair
With a sprig of peacock feathers in her hair,
María Luisa mounted on Marcial—
The eighteenth century rational ideal
Of measure and restraint met and perfected,
The reins of reason holding in the horses
That threaten to haul the carriage off the road.
But Goya knew the driver is a madman,
Knew pointed dunce caps of the Inquisition
And captives shot against a wall were proof:
Despite how civilized an age may seem,
The dream of reason is just another dream.

3.

At night when Goya stands beside my bed
Demanding that I answer for my dreams
And swearing to heaven that he is not dead
You turn the lamp on, wakened by my screams
And say there is no need to be afraid.
But I have seen the horse without a rider
Charging the battlefield and dead men flayed
Down to the gristle where the fat turns whiter,
Seen heretics bound fast against a stake
And set on fire to light the fevered dark
Before a jeering crowd, for Jesus' sake . . .
The nightmare wets its brush and leaves its mark:
A scintilla of insanity, a smutch
Behind the eyes where reason cannot touch.

4.

The spider—architect and artist—tiptoes
Across the dew-wet thread that it has spun
Between the silk tree and the windowpane.
Awake on restless summer nights like these,
I play old country songs and look at Goya.
I thumb through Saturn, madhouse, matador,
The milk-skinned maja lounging in the raw,
And wait for dawn to rise above the trees
Until you fetch me back to bed. See how
The strange and beautiful lie down together:
Colossus strides above the killing fields
While Patsy Cline sings "Back in Baby's Arms."
The spider, like a scholar lost in thought,
Broods on the shrouded housefly it has caught.

5.

Watching the blackbirds gather on the lawn,
I stand outside and think of Goya's words
Etched in metal, *El sueño de la razon*—
And everywhere I see the circling birds
Of sheer unreason: wars and rumors of wars
And demagogues who traffic in derision,
Feasts and fashion while Lazarus licks his sores,
Divided governments mired in indecision,
Riots and rape and racial violence,
Dried up rivers and spiking temperatures
And bought officials who bury evidence
With whispers, empty oaths, and signatures,
The well-heeled, hands out, clamoring for more …
I go back in the house and slam the door.

6.

Goya walks down the moon-washed avenues
At midnight past the houses and the crowds.
The spark of terror sputters on its fuse
And starlight disappears behind the clouds.
I stand at the window watching as he leans
To sketch a dead child clutched in Saturn's claw,
Shootings and shipwrecks, demons, and machines
Of torture, a sheep carcass flensed and raw—
And when he turns to stand outside my door,
He holds his sketch book up for me to see
The roots, exposed, that burrow at the core
Deep as a nerve and won't let go of me:
Those phantoms, appetites, and fantasies
That pulse in the human brain like a disease.

7.

What Goya knew of suffering could fill
Ten volumes with material to spare.
I have known suffering. You sometimes speak
Of those long years the black dog rode my back
And mania would keep me up for weeks,
The raving speech and the rage that nearly broke us.
When I think about the nights I could not sleep,
How I paced the kitchen floor or punched the drywall
While you lay there alone upstairs in bed,
I think of Goya, deaf, trapped in his head,
The sleep of reason that produces monsters
Driving him to set down those images
Of leering lunatics I can still see.
I look at them with fear. They look at me.

8.

The world goes down in blood and it is Goya:
Goya in toppled towers, feuds and factions,
In crime and crowded jails and genocide,
Goya in the collusions and conspiracies,
The whispers from the lips of history
Echoing in the streets and in the markets,
Goya in the struggles of the stricken,
The wars and scandals fixed on every tongue,
Goya in missiles, mines, and ammunition
Exploding down the routine routes of empire,
Goya in seeds of discord, superstition,
And rumors rising to riot and reaction,
Goya in hunger choking on a crumb,
Goya then, now, and in the age to come.

9.

Against the terrible dream of history
I set the present moment, new and near.
Here is the French bread waiting on its plate,
The white wine in its glass. Let Goya, deaf,
Bear witness to the midnight executions,
The monsters and mayhem of a brutal age.
His owls above the sleeper beat the air.
And if our times seem likewise, if the minds
Keenest with wisdom sink into despair,
At least for now the stars burn on the window
Where you sit musing at your own reflection—
The stars that shone on Pericles and Caesar,
Napoleon and Nero, and will shine on
In their indifferent fury when we are gone.

A Stroll in Summer

Japanese folding screen

They look like nothing
Else, the mountain and thin trees,
    The swags of cirrus

That billow above
The strollers climbing the slope
    To the green summit.

And the ancient sun
Is like a measure of thought
    Sweeping the valley

With its raw ochre,
A light of mere appearance
    That illuminates

The shapes and colors
And makes each particular
    Shine as from within.

This Japanese screen
Is the shadow of the world
    Set down on paper,

Summer brought indoors
And unfolded in a room.
    Timeless paradigm,

It is the high peak
Of the maker's dream, toward
    Which the strollers climb.

A Note About the Author

Photo courtesy of Megan Van Fleet © 2013

Morri Creech is the author of three collections of poetry, *Paper Cathedrals* (Kent State UP, 2001), *Field Knowledge* (Waywiser, 2006), which received the Anthony Hecht Poetry prize and was nominated for both the *Los Angeles Times Book Award* and the Poet's Prize, and *The Sleep of Reason* (Waywiser, March 2013), which was a finalist for the 2014 Pulitzer Prize. A recipient of NEA and Ruth Lilly Fellowships, as well as grants from the North Carolina and Louisiana Arts Councils, he is the Writer in Residence at Queens University of Charlotte, where he teaches courses in both the undergraduate creative writing program and in the low residency M.F.A. program. He lives in Charlotte, North Carolina with the novelist Sarah Creech and their two children.

Other Books from Waywiser

* Co-published with Picador

www.ingramcontent.com/pod-product-compliance
Lightning Source LLC
Chambersburg PA
CBHW071109090426
42737CB00013B/2549